JAPANESE FOR BUSY PEOPLE I
The Workbook for the Revised 3rd Edition

JAPANESE FOR BUSY PEOPLE

I

The Workbook
for the Revised 3rd Edition

Association for Japanese-Language Teaching
AjALT

KODANSHA INTERNATIONAL
Tokyo • New York • London

The Association for Japanese-Language Teaching (AJALT) was recognized as a nonprofit organization by the Ministry of Education in 1977. It was established to meet the practical needs of people who are not necessarily specialists on Japan but who wish to communicate effectively in Japanese. In 1992 AJALT was awarded the Japan Foundation Special Prize. AJALT maintains a website at www.ajalt.org, through which they can be contacted with questions regarding this book or any of their other publications.

Illustrations by Shinsaku Sumi

CD narration by Yuki Minatsuki, Aya Ogawa, Yuri Haruta, Koji Yoshida, Tatsuo Endo, Sosei Shinbori, and Howard Colefield

CD recording and editing by The English Language Education Council, Inc.

Distributed in the United States by Kodansha America, Inc., and in the United Kingdom and continental Europe by Kodansha Europe Ltd.

Published by Kodansha International Ltd., 17–14 Otowa 1-chome, Bunkyo-ku, Tokyo 112–8652, and Kodansha America, Inc.

First published 1993
Second edition 1994
Third edition 2006
15 14 13 12 11 10 09 08   12 11 10 9 8 7 6 5 4 3

CONTENTS

INTRODUCTION

Aims and Features of the Workbook

This workbook has been designed to meet the needs of students who have studied Japanese but cannot yet speak it comfortably. It can be used both inside the classroom and outside of it, in tandem with *Japanese for Busy People I: Revised 3rd Edition* or as independent study material. It can also provide a good review for those learners who have completed the equivalent of the first half of a typical first-year course but feel dissatisfied with their speaking abilities. In short, it is fit for all learners who wish to improve their speaking skills, regardless of their learning environment.

Ample Speaking Practice

The workbook consists of exercises, short dialogues, and target dialogues from *Japanese for Busy People I: Revised 3rd Edition* (some revised and expanded), as well as new review sections, all with illustrations that allow learners to vividly envision themselves in each situation as they practice. The dialogues are designed to help learners acquire the skills to carry on appropriate conversations in everyday situations.

The ability to speak well comes not merely through an understanding of grammar and vocabulary but through repeated oral practice, in the same way that learning to play the piano is more than learning how to move one's fingers. Keep this in mind as you make use of this workbook to advance your study of Japanese.

Fun and Lively Practice through Audio Recordings and Pictures

Dialogue practice needs to feel realistic in order to be effective. This workbook employs audio recordings and illustrations to help make learners feel as if they are actually experiencing each situation. In what is one of the advantages of pictures over words, we also use illustrations in this book to visually point out information that cannot be conveyed as well verbally, for example how and at what point to bow in the midst of a conversation.

Practicing Listening and Responding

Real-life conversations require participants not only to speak but also to listen. Both listening and speaking skills are necessary for one to correctly understand what the other party is saying, communicate one's own thoughts in response, and wait for the ball to be tossed back again from the other side.

The workbook focuses on nurturing such "listening and responding" skills. Listening skills cannot be developed simply through silently following letters on a page. Be sure to listen to the attached CD many times and accustom yourself to the natural speed and standard intonation and accents of the Japanese recorded there by professionally trained speakers.

Easy Self-Practice

Although speaking practice is nearly impossible without someone to talk to, most learners studying by themselves are not so lucky as to have a conversation partner on hand. In the recordings of the conversations on the CD, the lines of the non-Japanese characters—Mr. Smith, Ms. Chan, Mr. Green, and so on—are left out of the target dialogues, and parts of the short dialogues ("key phrases") are left unspoken, too, to enable learners to practice the blank parts on their own. By relying on the CD as a trusty guide, learners will come to naturally acquire the rhythms and sensibilities of Japanese conversation.

How to Use the Workbook

The workbook is made up of 25 lessons, the content of which has been drawn from the lessons in *Japanese for Busy People I: Revised 3rd Edition*. Each lesson is made up of one or two exercises, one or two short dialogues, and a target dialogue, all excerpted from the main text. (Some dialogues have been adapted and/or expanded to fit the needs of the workbook.) In addition, the book features review pages, including one comprehensive review at the end.

Exercises

The exercises are based on the conversation practice exercises (marked by a 🎧 icon) in the main textbook (Book I). (In some cases the dialogues have been adapted and/or expanded to fit the needs of the workbook.) Each exercise consists of an illustration with the appropriate Japanese expressions left blank, a dialogue that shows exactly what is being said, and two or three numbered illustrations at the bottom of the page.

1) Refer to the illustration as you listen along on the CD and try to grasp the basic content of the dialogue, for example who did what where and when.

2) Without listening to the CD, reconstruct the dialogue line by line, taking hints from the illustrations and the words provided. Try not to look at the text beneath the cartoon.

3) Practice the dialogue until you can speak all the lines fluently.

4) Practice the dialogue some more, this time by reading the text and replacing the underlined parts with the Japanese words suggested by each of the numbered illustrations given. The answers are at the back of the book.

The short dialogues introduce useful idioms and other common expressions. These expressions are taken up separately on the CD, at the beginning of the track, to enable listeners to first practice them before putting them to use.

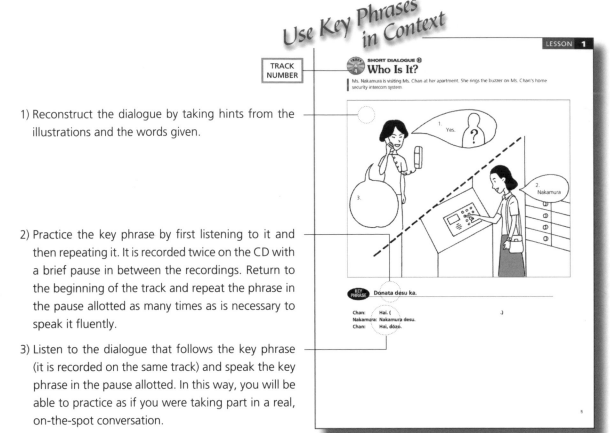

1) Reconstruct the dialogue by taking hints from the illustrations and the words given.

2) Practice the key phrase by first listening to it and then repeating it. It is recorded twice on the CD with a brief pause in between the recordings. Return to the beginning of the track and repeat the phrase in the pause allotted as many times as is necessary to speak it fluently.

3) Listen to the dialogue that follows the key phrase (it is recorded on the same track) and speak the key phrase in the pause allotted. In this way, you will be able to practice as if you were taking part in a real, on-the-spot conversation.

NOTE: Complete recordings of the short dialogues, including the parts left blank, are available on the CD for *Japanese for Busy People I, Revised 3rd Edition*.

How to Listen and Practice

For effective listening practice, try the following techniques.

REPETITION: After first listening to the speaker, repeat what was said how it was said.

SHADOWING: Repeat what is being said a little behind the speaker, just like you would if you were doing simultaneous interpretation.

OVERLAPPING: Say the lines along with the speaker, emulating not only pronunciation but also accent and intonation to achieve perfect unison.

DICTATION: Listen to the speaker and accurately write down what is being said.

The target dialogues, like the exercises and short dialogues in this book, come with illustrations that depict the scenarios presented in them. The CD includes (1) a full recording of the dialogue and (2) a recording with the parts of the non-Japanese speaker left out. The conversation proceeds at a natural pace, leaving learners little time to mentally translate from their native language or to fish for the right particle or verb conjugation. Through repeated practice of the target dialogues, learners will come to acquire the rhythms of real-life Japanese conversation.

Talk Like a Native Speaker

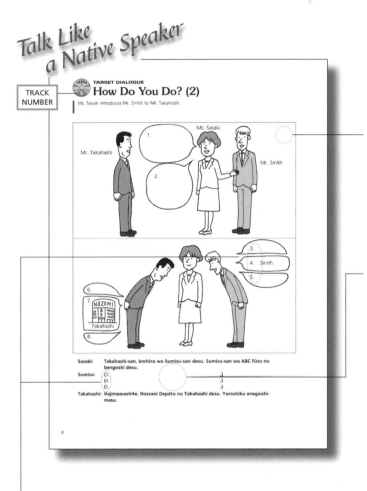

TRACK NUMBER

1) Reconstruct the dialogue by taking hints from the illustrations and the words given. Again, try to avoid looking at the text beneath the illustration.

2) Listen to the CD and compare your dialogue to the one recorded. Make changes to your own dialogue as necessary.

3) Act out the parts of the non-Japanese speaker using the recording (found on the same track) in which his or her parts are left unspoken. Practice until you can utter the speaker's lines smoothly within the pauses allotted without stopping the CD.

The numbers here correspond.

The review pages appear every few lessons and call on learners to make up dialogues using the vocabulary and sentence patterns they have practiced up to that point. Look at the illustrations and, taking hints from the English provided, act out the dialogues in Japanese. Sample dialogues are provided in the Answers section at the back of the book.

Acknowledgments for *Japanese for Busy People I: The Workbook* (2nd edition, 1994)

This book was prepared by Akiko Kajikawa and Junko Shinada, teachers at AJALT, with the advice of Shigeko Miyazaki, Miyako Iwami, and Haruko Matsui, and the assistance of Yoko Hattori, Hiroko Kuroda, and Harumi Mizuno, all of whom are AJALT teachers. This workbook made use of numerous illustrations that have contributed to the book's effectiveness as a learning resource. Many of its exercises were incorporated into *Japanese for Busy People I, Revised 3rd Edition.*

Acknowledgments for *Japanese for Busy People I: The Workbook for the Revised 3rd Edition*

We the authors would like to sincerely thank Shinsaku Sumi, our illustrator, who responded to our many demands by coming up with wonderful pictures that will no doubt make our readers feel excited and eager to learn Japanese.

This workbook was supervised by Izumi Sawa and written by five AJALT instructors, Erino Ido, Yoshiko Okubo, Yuko Takami, Hirohiko Matsuoka, and Chikako Watanabe. Many other AJALT instructors are also to be thanked for all their support, advice, and encouragement during the development of these learning materials.

THE WORKBOOK

EXERCISE ①

This Is Mr. Smith

Mr. Green introduces Mr. Smith and Ms. Sasaki to each other.

Gurin: Kochira wa Sumisu-san desu. Kochira wa <u>Sasaki-san</u> desu.
Sumisu: Hajimemashite. Sumisu desu. Yoroshiku onegaishimasu.
Sasaki: Hajimemashite. <u>Sasaki</u> desu. Yoroshiku onegaishimasu.

①  Mr. Kato

②  Ms. Nakamura

③  Mr. Suzuki

④  Ms. Chan

TRACK 2 **EXERCISE Ⅱ**
How Do You Do? (1)

Ms. Chan introduces her friend to Ms. Nakamura.

ex.

1. Mr. Nattaporn

2.

3. ABC Foods Nakamura

4.

5.

6. Bangkok Airlines Nattaporn

7.

Chan: Kochira wa <u>Nattapon-san</u> desu.
Nakamura: Hajimemashite. ABC Fūzu no Nakamura desu. Yoroshiku onegaishimasu.
Nattapon: Hajimemashite. <u>Bankoku Kōkū no Nattapon</u> desu. Yoroshiku onegaishimasu.

①
Mr. Gibson
Australia Embassy

②
Ms. Park
Korea Trading

③
Ms. White
Canada Securities

④
Mr. Fernandez
Spain Insurance

NEW WORDS

kōkū	airlines
taishikan	embassy
bōeki	trading
shōken	securities
hoken	insurance

TRACK 3 **SHORT DIALOGUE ①**
Mr. Takahashi, Please

Mr. Smith is visiting Nozomi Department Store. He arrives at the reception desk.

1.
ABC Foods
Smith

2.
Mr. Takahashi, please.

3.

KEY PHRASE **Takahashi-san o onegaishimasu.**

Sumisu: ABC Fūzu no Sumisu desu. (.)
uketsuke: Hai.

SHORT DIALOGUE ⑪
Who Is It?

Ms. Nakamura is visiting Ms. Chan at her apartment. She rings the buzzer on Ms. Chan's home security intercom system.

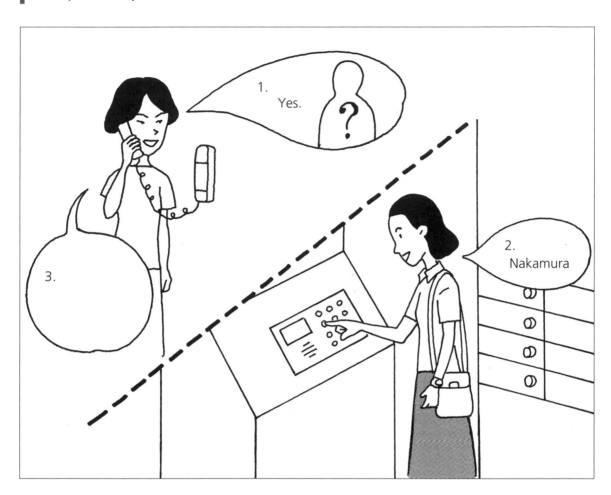

KEY PHRASE   **Donata desu ka.**

Chan: **Hai. (.)**
Nakamura: **Nakamura desu.**
Chan: **Hai, dōzo.**

TARGET DIALOGUE

How Do You Do? (2)

Ms. Sasaki introduces Mr. Smith to Mr. Takahashi.

Sasaki: Takahashi-san, kochira wa Sumisu-san desu. Sumisu-san wa ABC Fūzu no bengoshi desu.

Sumisu: (3.   .)
(4.   .)
(5.   .)

Takahashi: Hajimemashite. Nozomi Depāto no Takahashi desu. Yoroshiku onegaishi-masu.

EXERCISE
Is This Your Umbrella?

After a meeting, Mr. Smith finds an umbrella, so he asks Mr. Suzuki about it.

Sumisu: Kore wa Suzuki-san no <u>kasa</u> desu ka.

Suzuki: Iie, watashi no dewa arimasen.

Sumisu: Dare no <u>kasa</u> desu ka.

Suzuki: Chan-san no desu.

SHORT DIALOGUE ①
Is This Your Date Book?

TRACK 7

Mr. Smith and Mr. Takahashi have just had a meeting. After Mr. Takahashi leaves the room, Mr. Smith finds a date book on the sofa.

KEY PHRASE   **Kore wa Nakamura-san no techō desu ka.**

Sumisu:	(.)
Nakamura:	Iie, watashi no dewa arimasen.
Sumisu:	Dare no desu ka.
Nakamura:	(*noticing Mr. Takahashi's name on the date book, Ms. Nakamura runs after him*)
	Kore wa Takahashi-san no techō desu ka.
Takahashi:	Ee, sō desu. Dōmo arigatō gozaimasu.

SHORT DIALOGUE ⑪
Could You Repeat That?

TRACK 8

Ms. Chan meets Mrs. Matsui at a party and asks her for her telephone number.

KEY PHRASE   **Sumimasen. Mō ichi-do onegaishimasu.**

Chan: Matsui-san no denwa-bangō wa nan-ban desu ka.
Matsui: 03-3459-9630 desu. Keitai wa 090-1234-5678 desu.
Chan: (.)

TARGET DIALOGUE
Is This Your Name?

Mr. Takahashi gives Mr. Smith his business card. Mr. Smith cannot read kanji.

Takahashi:	**Watashi no meishi desu. Dōzo.**
Sumisu:	(2. .)
	(*flipping over Takahashi's business card to examine the other side*)
	(3. .)
Takahashi:	**Ee, sō desu. Takahashi Shingo desu.**
Sumisu:	(5. .)
Takahashi:	**Kaisha no namae desu. Nozomi Depāto desu.**

EXERCISE

What Time Is Dinner?

Ms. Chan is at a resort hotel. She is asking the front desk about the hours of the hotel's services.

Chan: Sumimasen. Ban-gohan wa nan-ji kara desu ka.
furonto: 6-ji kara desu.
Chan: Dōmo arigatō.

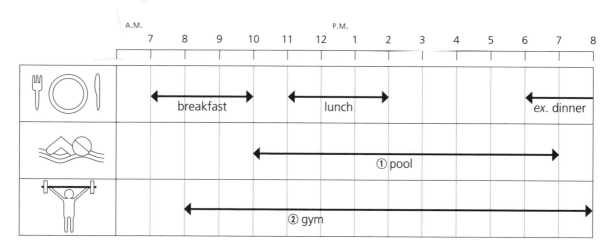

TRACK 11

SHORT DIALOGUE

What Time Is It in London Now?

Ms. Sasaki wants to call the London branch of her company.

KEY PHRASE Rondon wa ima nan-ji desu ka.

Sasaki:	Nakamura-san, ima nan-ji desu ka.
Nakamura:	4-ji han desu.
Sasaki:	(.)
Nakamura:	Gozen 8-ji han desu.
Sasaki:	Sō desu ka. Dōmo arigatō.

TRACK 12

TARGET DIALOGUE

What Time Do They Open?

Mr. Smith goes to the department store, but it isn't open yet.

Sumisu: (1. .)
onna no hito: 9-ji 50-pun desu.
Sumisu: (3. .)
onna no hito: 10-ji kara desu.
Sumisu: (5. .)
onna no hito: Gogo 8-ji made desu.
Sumisu: (7. .)
onna no hito: Dō itashimashite.

EXERCISE
Is That a CD Player?

Mr. Smith is in an electronics store. He wants to know what certain items are and how much they cost.

Sumisu:	Sumimasen. Are wa **CD-purēyā** desu ka.
mise no hito:	Iie, **rajio** desu.
Sumisu:	Sore wa **CD-purēyā** desu ka.
mise no hito:	Hai, sō desu.
Sumisu:	Ikura desu ka.
mise no hito:	**23,000-en** desu.
Sumisu:	Ja, sore o kudasai.

①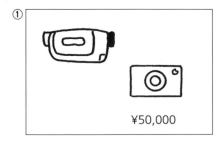

¥50,000

②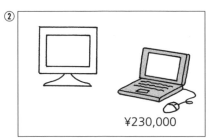

¥230,000

TRACK
14

SHORT DIALOGUE
Can I Pay by Credit Card?

Mr. Smith is at a store, shopping.

KEY PHRASE   Kādo demo ii desu ka.

Sumisu: Kore o kudasai.
mise no hito: 4,300-en desu.
Sumisu: (.)
mise no hito: Hai, kekkō desu.

TARGET DIALOGUE
How Much Is This One?

Mr. Smith is shopping in a department store.

mise no hito: **Irasshaimase.**
Sumisu: *(pointing)* **(2.   .)**
mise no hito: **Hai, dōzo.**
Sumisu: **(4.   .)**
mise no hito: **3,000-en desu.**
Sumisu: *(pointing)* **(6.   .)**
mise no hito: **Kore mo 3,000-en desu.**
Sumisu: **(8.   .)**
mise no hito: **Hai, arigatō gozaimasu.**

TRACK 16

EXERCISE

How Much Is That Towel? Where Is It From?

Ms. Chan wants to know the price and country of origin of certain items in a store where she is shopping.

Chan:	Sumimasen. Sono <u>taoru</u> wa ikura desu ka.
mise no hito:	1,500-en desu.
Chan:	Sore wa doko no <u>taoru</u> desu ka.
mise no hito:	<u>Furansu</u> no desu.
Chan:	Ja, sore o <u>6-mai</u> kudasai.

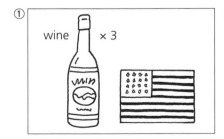

① wine × 3

② coffee cup × 4

TRACK 17 **SHORT DIALOGUE**
Three Cream Puffs, Please

Ms. Chan is at a confectionary. She wants to buy some cream puffs.

KEY PHRASE   **Shūkurīmu o mittsu kudasai.**

mise no hito: Irasshaimase.
Chan: (.)
mise no hito: Hai. 630-en desu.

TARGET DIALOGUE

How Much Is That Red T-shirt?

Mr. Smith is shopping for a T-shirt.

Sumisu:	(1.	.)
mise no hito:	**Dore desu ka.**	
Sumisu:	(3.	.)
mise no hito:	**Are wa 1,500-en desu.**	
Sumisu:	(5.	.)
mise no hito:	**1,000-en desu.**	
Sumisu:	(7.	.)

Mr. Takahashi meets Ms. Brown for the first time.

Ms. Chan is shopping for a digital camera.

TRACK 19

EXERCISE

I'll Go with Ms. Sasaki

Mr. Smith is talking on the phone with a person from the Osaka branch office.

Ōsaka-shisha no hito:	Sumisu-san wa itsu Ōsaka-shisha ni kimasu ka.
Sumisu:	<u>Ashita</u> ikimasu.
Ōsaka-shisha no hito:	Dare to kimasu ka.
Sumisu:	<u>Sasaki-san</u> to ikimasu.
Ōsaka-shisha no hito:	Sō desu ka.

① next week

Ms.Chan

② the day after tomorrow

Mr.Kato

SHORT DIALOGUE ①
Have a Nice Trip

Ms. Chan sees Mr. Suzuki in front of ABC Foods carrying a large piece of luggage.

KEY PHRASE   **Itterasshai.**

Chan: **A, Suzuki-san, shutchō desu ka.**
Suzuki: **Ee, Ōsaka-shisha ni ikimasu. Asatte Tōkyō ni kaerimasu.**
Chan: **Sō desu ka. (**   **.)**

SHORT DIALOGUE ⑪
Does This Bus Go to Shibuya?

At a bus stop, Mr. Smith asks the driver a question before boarding.

 Kono basu wa Shibuya ni ikimasu ka.

Sumisu:	Sumimasen. (....)
basu no untenshu:	Iie, ikimasen.
Sumisu:	Dono basu ga ikimasu ka.
basu no untenshu:	88-ban no basu ga ikimasu.
Sumisu:	Arigatō gozaimasu.

TRACK 22

TARGET DIALOGUE
I'll Go to Your Company Tomorrow

Mr. Smith phones Mr. Takahashi of Nozomi Department Store to confirm the time of Friday's meeting.

Sumisu:	(1.	.)
Takahashi:	Takahashi desu. Ohayō gozaimasu.	
Sumisu:	(3.	.)
Takahashi:	Hai, 3-ji kara desu. Hitori de kimasu ka.	
Sumisu:	(6.	.)
Takahashi:	Sō desu ka. Dewa, ashita.	
Sumisu:	(8.	.)

EXERCISE
I'll Go by Shinkansen

Ms. Chan and someone from the Kyoto branch office of ABC Foods are confirming the schedule for the branch-office employee's visit to the Tokyo office.

Kyōto-shisha no hito:	Raishū no getsu-yōbi ni sochira ni ikimasu.
Chan:	Nan-ji ni kimasu ka.
Kyōto-shisha no hito:	<u>9-ji</u> ni ikimasu.
Chan:	Nan de kimasu ka.
Kyōto-shisha no hito:	<u>Shinkansen</u> de ikimasu.
Chan:	Sō desu ka.

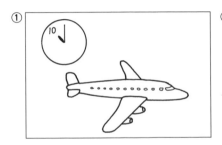

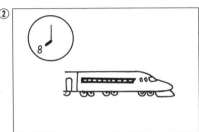

SHORT DIALOGUE
I Came from Hong Kong Last October

Mr. Takahashi and Ms. Chan are having tea at Nozomi Department Store.

KEY PHRASE   Kyonen no 10-gatsu ni Honkon kara kimashita.

Takahashi: Chan-san wa itsu Nihon ni kimashita ka.
Chan: (.)
Takahashi: Sō desu ka. Natsu-yasumi ni Honkon ni kaerimasu ka.
Chan: Iie, kaerimasen. Tomodachi to Okinawa ni ikimasu.

TARGET DIALOGUE
I Came by Subway

Mr. Smith goes with Ms. Chan to Nozomi Department Store on business.

Takahashi:	Sumisu-san, Chan-san, dōzo ohairikudasai.
Sumisu:	(2. .)
Chan:	Shitsureishimasu.
Takahashi:	Dōzo kochira e.
Sumisu, Chan:	(5. .)
Takahashi:	Kuruma de kimashita ka.
Sumisu:	(7. .)

EXERCISE

TRACK
26

There Are Shrines and Temples in Kamakura

Ms. Nakamura is telling Mr. Smith about her plans for the weekend.

Nakamura: **Nichi-yōbi ni kuruma de <u>Kamakura</u> ni ikimasu.**
Sumisu: **Sō desu ka. <u>Kamakura</u> ni nani ga arimasu ka.**
Nakamura: **<u>Jinja ya o-tera</u> ga arimasu.**
Sumisu: **Ii desu ne.**

① Odaiba
spa / HOTEL / etc.

② Hakone
hot springs / lake etc.

SHORT READING

There's a Soba Restaurant Next to the Inn

Mr. Kato is describing the surroundings of the famous inn he stayed at in Nikko.

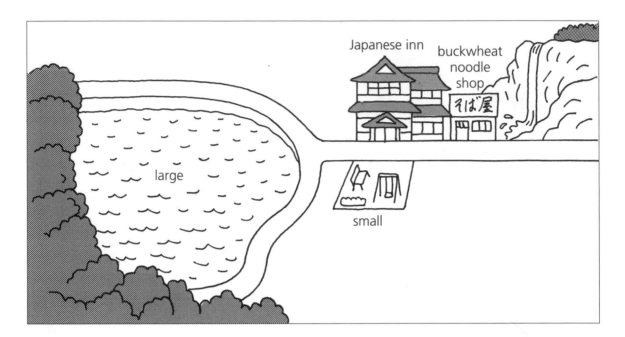

KEY PHRASE   **Ryokan no tonari ni soba-ya ga arimasu.**

Ryokan no chikaku ni ōkii mizuumi ya taki ga arimasu.
(.)
Ryokan no mae ni chiisai kōen ga arimasu.

TARGET DIALOGUE
What's in Nikko?

Mr. Kato and Ms. Chan are talking about Nikko.

Katō: Do-yōbi ni kazoku to Nikkō ni ikimasu.

Chan: (2.   .)

Katō: Ōkii o-tera ya jinja ga arimasu. Onsen mo arimasu.

Chan: (5.   .)

Katō: (*shows her a pamphlet and points*) **Kore desu. Nihon no supa desu yo.**

Chan: (8.   .)

EXERCISE

The Bus Stop Is in Front of the Station

Mr. Smith is looking for a bus stop.

Sumisu: Sumimasen. Kono chikaku ni <u>basu-noriba</u> ga arimasu ka.
onna no hito: Ee, arimasu yo.
Sumisu: Doko desu ka.
onna no hito: <u>Basu-noriba</u> wa <u>eki no mae</u> desu.
Sumisu: Dōmo arigatō gozaimasu.

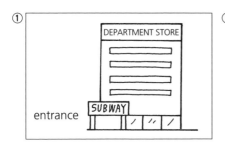

① entrance

② bus stop

SHORT DIALOGUE ①
Here You Go

Mr. Kato is looking for today's newspaper.

KEY PHRASE **Hai, dōzo.**

Katō: **Kyō no shimbun wa doko ni arimasu ka.**
Chan: **Koko ni arimasu. (** .)

SHORT DIALOGUE ⑪
Where Are You Right Now?

Mr. Kato calls Mr. Suzuki on his cell phone while Mr. Suzuki is out on a sales visit.

KEY PHRASE   **Ima doko desu ka.**

Katō: Suzuki-san. (.)
Suzuki: Ima Nozomi Depāto ni imasu.
Katō: Nan-ji goro kaisha ni kaerimasu ka.
Suzuki: 3-ji ni kaerimasu.

TARGET DIALOGUE
Where's the Parking Lot?

Mr. Kato has come to Nikko. He asks a salesperson at a store where to find a parking lot.

Katō:	(1. .)
mise no hito:	Ee. Arimasu yo.
Katō:	(3. .)
mise no hito:	Asoko ni kombini ga arimasu ne. Chūshajō wa ano kombini no tonari desu.
Katō:	(6. .)

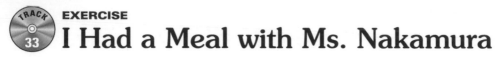

EXERCISE

I Had a Meal with Ms. Nakamura

Mr. Suzuki asks Ms. Chan what she did over the weekend.

ex.

1. last weekend
2. Ms. Nakamura
3. where ?
4. Ginza
5.

Suzuki: **Shūmatsu ni nani o shimashita ka.**
Chan: **Nakamura-san to shokuji o shimashita.**
Suzuki: **Doko de shimashita ka.**
Chan: **Ginza de shimashita.**
Suzuki: **Sō desu ka.**

① friend
Shibuya

② Mr.Smith
Hakone

SHORT DIALOGUE
I'd Like to Make a Reservation, Please

Mr. Suzuki phones the tempura specialty restaurant Tenmasa to make a reservation.

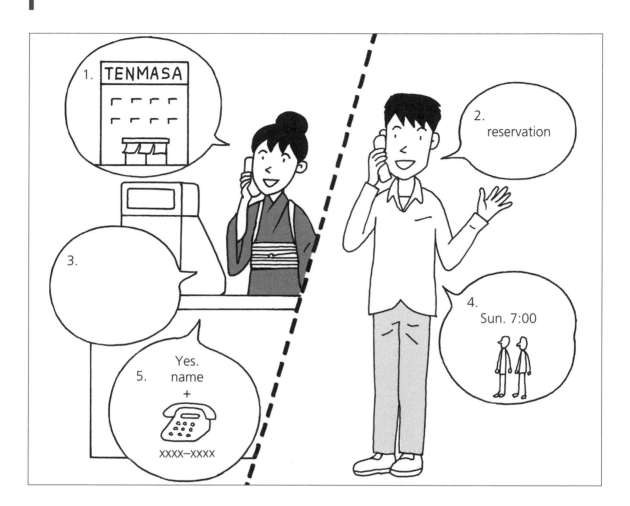

KEY PHRASE   **Yoyaku o onegaishimasu.**

mise no hito: **Temmasa de gozaimasu.**
Suzuki: (.)
mise no hito: **Hai, arigatō gozaimasu.**
Suzuki: **Nichi-yōbi no 7-ji ni onegaishimasu. Futari desu.**
mise no hito: **Hai, wakarimashita. Dewa, o-namae to o-denwa-bangō o onegaishimasu.**

TARGET DIALOGUE
What Will You Do This Weekend?

Ms. Sasaki and Mr. Smith are talking about their plans for the weekend.

Sumisu: (1.   .)

Sasaki: Do-yōbi ni tomodachi to Kabuki o mimasu.

Sumisu: (3.   .)

Sasaki: Sumisu-san wa?

Sumisu: (5.   .)

Sasaki: Ii desu ne.

TRACK
36

EXERCISE
Do You Often Go to the Gym?

Mr. Suzuki asks Mr. Smith what he will do this coming weekend.

Suzuki: **Kondo no shūmatsu ni nani o shimasu ka.**

Sumisu: **ABC Supōtsu-kurabu ni ikimasu.**

Suzuki: **Sumisu-san wa yoku ABC Supōtsu-kurabu ni ikimasu ka.**

Sumisu: **Ee, mashīn ga takusan arimasu kara.**

①

department store
in Ginza

②

English video

Tokyo Library

TRACK 37

SHORT DIALOGUE ①

Two Draft Beers, Please

Mr. Green comes to the restaurant Tenmasa with his wife.

KEY PHRASE Nama-bīru o futatsu onegaishimasu.

Gurīn:	Sumimasen. Matsu-kōsu o futatsu onegaishimasu.
mise no hito:	Hai. O-nomimono wa?
Gurīn:	(.)
mise no hito:	Hai.

SHORT DIALOGUE ⑪
Check, Please

Mr. Green pays for his meal at Tenmasa and asks for a receipt.

KEY PHRASE   O-kanjō o onegaishimasu.

Gurin:	Sumimasen. (.)
mise no hito:	Hai.
Gurin:	Sumimasen. Ryōshūsho o onegaishimasu.
mise no hito:	Hai. O-namae wa?

TARGET DIALOGUE
Do You Come to This Restaurant Often?

Mr. Smith and Mr. Suzuki have arrived at a tempura restaurant in Ginza.

mise no hito:	Irasshaimase.
Suzuki:	**Suzuki desu.**
mise no hito:	**Suzuki-sama desu ne. Dōzo kochira e.**
Sumisu:	*(a few moments later, at the table)*
	(4. .)
	(5. .)
Suzuki:	**Ee, tokidoki kimasu. Oishii desu kara.**
Sumisu:	*(fifteen minutes later, after their dishes have arrived)*
	(8. .)
Suzuki:	**Kisu desu.**
Sumisu:	**(10. .)**

Describe Mr. Smith's life in Tokyo.

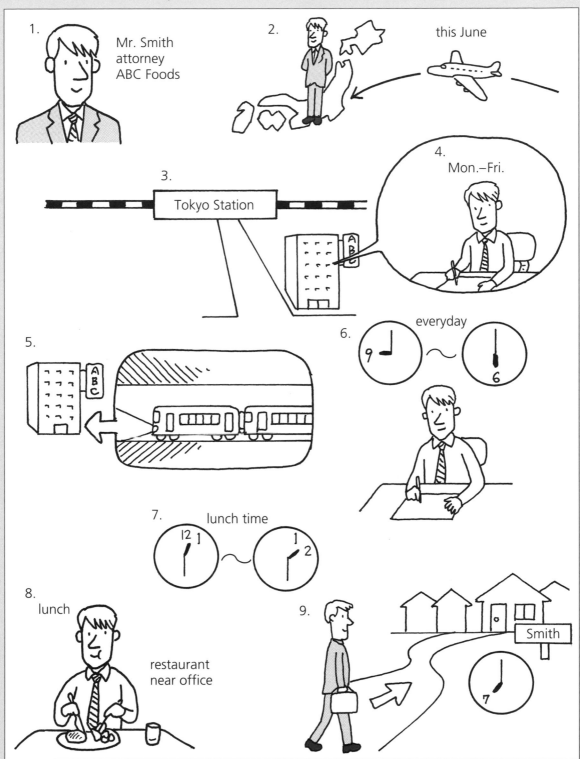

1. Mr. Smith
   attorney
   ABC Foods

2. this June

3. Tokyo Station

4. Mon.–Fri.

5.

6. everyday

7. lunch time

8. lunch
   restaurant
   near office

9. Smith

EXERCISE ①
It's Cold Today, Isn't It?

Ms. Chan and Ms. Sasaki chat about the weather.

ex.

1. today
2. Yes.

Chan: Kyō wa <u>samui</u> desu ne.
Sasaki: Ee, hontō ni <u>samui</u> desu ne.

①

②

good weather

③

warm

④

cool

NEW WORDS

atatakai   warm
suzushii   cool

TRACK 41

EXERCISE 11
Is the Taxi Stand Far from Here?

Mr. Smith asks a woman on the street about the location of a taxi stand he is looking for.

Sumisu: Sumimasen. <u>Takushī-noriba</u> wa koko kara tōi desu ka.
onna no hito: Iie, tōkunai desu. Aruite 5-fun gurai desu yo.
Sumisu: Sō desu ka. Arigatō gozaimasu.

①

②

SHORT DIALOGUE ①
May I Come In?

Mr. Smith visits Mr. Takahashi's home. He rings the security system intercom.

KEY PHRASE   Ojamashimasu.

_____

Takahashi: **Hai.**
Sumisu: **Sumisu desu.**
Takahashi: **A, chotto matte kudasai.** (*Takahashi goes to answer the door.*)
Takahashi: **Yoku irasshaimashita.**
Sumisu: (.)

TRACK 43

SHORT DIALOGUE ⑪
It's a Little Bit Expensive, Isn't It?

Mr. Smith is at an antique shop in Tokyo.

KEY PHRASE **Chotto takai desu ne.**

Sumisu:	Kore wa ikura desu ka.
mise no hito:	8,000-en desu.
Sumisu:	(.)
mise no hito:	Kore wa 6,500-en desu.
Sumisu:	Ja, sore o kudasai.

TARGET DIALOGUE
It's Very Delicious

Mr. Smith has been invited to the home of his client Mr. Takahashi for the first time.

Takahashi:	**O-cha o dōzo.**
Sumisu:	(2. .)
Takahashi:	**O-kashi wa ikaga desu ka.**
Sumisu:	(4. .)
	(5. .)
	(6. .)
Takahashi:	**Ee, sō desu.**
Sumisu:	(8. .)
Takahashi:	**O-cha o mō 1-pai ikaga desu ka.**
Sumisu:	(10. .)

TRACK 45 **EXERCISE**
I Got It for My Birthday (1)

Ms. Nakamura is wearing a new scarf.

ex.
1. scarf
2. friend
3. It looks good on you.
4.

Sumisu:	<u>Kireina sukāfu</u> desu ne.
Nakamura:	Ee, <u>tanjōbi</u> ni tomodachi ni moraimashita.
Sumisu:	Yoku niaimasu ne.
Nakamura:	Arigatō gozaimasu.

① good

②

SHORT DIALOGUE ①

Well, I'll Have to Be Leaving Soon

Mr. Smith is visiting Mr. Takahashi's house. Having been there for a few hours already, he glances at his watch, knowing he should get going soon.

1.

2. You're welcome.

KEY PHRASE Ja, sorosoro shitsureishimasu.

Sumisu: (.)
Kyō wa dōmo arigatō gozaimashita.
Takahashi: Dō itashimashite.

SHORT DIALOGUE ⓫

Please Have Some Peaches

Mrs. Matsui, who lives next door to the Greens, has received a bunch of peaches from a friend.
She brings some to Mrs. Green.

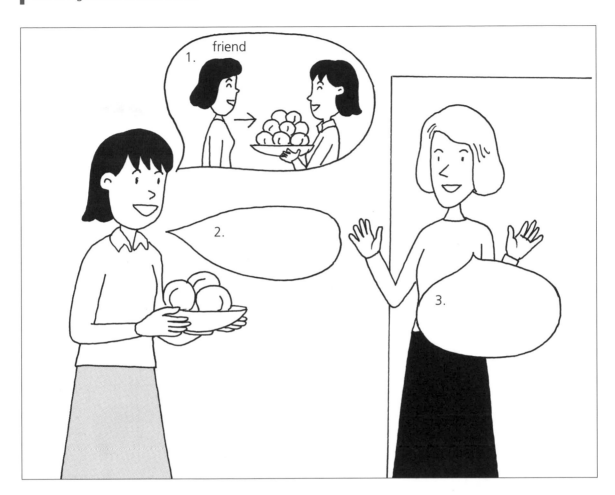

KEY PHRASE   **Kore, dōzo.**

Matsui: **Tomodachi ni momo o takusan moraimashita.**
       (.)
Gurin: **Dōmo arigatō gozaimasu.**

TARGET DIALOGUE

I Got It for My Birthday (2)

Mr. Takahashi and Mr. Smith are talking about the flower vase that Mr. Takahashi received from Ms. Hoffman.

Sumisu: (1.   .)

Takahashi: **Ee, tanjōbi ni tomodachi no Hofuman-san ni moraimashita.**

Sumisu: (3.   .)

Takahashi: **Ee, watashi no sukina iro desu.**

TRACK 49

EXERCISE ①
How Was Hakone?

Mr. Green went to Hakone over the weekend.

Gurīn: **Shūmatsu ni** <u>Hakone no onsen</u> **ni ikimashita. Kore,** <u>Hakone</u> **no o-miyage desu. Dōzo.**

Sasaki: **Arigatō gozaimasu.** <u>Hakone</u> **wa dō deshita ka.**

Gurīn: **Totemo** <u>tanoshikatta desu.</u>

①

②

EXERCISE ⑪

Is This the Sasakis' Residence?

Mr. Smith telephones Ms. Sasaki, but her husband answers the phone.

Sumisu:	Moshimoshi, <u>Sasaki-san</u> no o-taku desu ka.
Sasaki-san no go-shujin:	Hai, sō desu.
Sumisu:	Sumisu desu. <u>Okusan</u> wa irasshaimasu ka.
Sasaki-san no go-shujin:	Hai. Chotto o-machi kudasai.

TRACK 51 **SHORT DIALOGUE**

Thank You for the Peaches Yesterday

The morning after receiving some peaches from Mrs. Matsui, Mrs. Green happens to run into Mrs. Matsui. She thanks her for the peaches.

 KEY PHRASE **Kinō wa momo o arigatō gozaimashita.**

Gurin: **Ohayō gozaimasu.**
Matsui: **Ohayō gozaimasu.**
Gurin: **(** .) **Totemo oishikatta desu.**
Matsui: **Sō desu ka. Yokatta desu.**

TARGET DIALOGUE
It Was a Lot of Fun

Mr. Smith phones Mr. Takahashi the day after visiting his house. Before getting to the point of the call, he thanks Mr. Takahashi for his hospitality.

Sumisu:	(1. .)
Takahashi:	**Hai, sō desu.**
Sumisu:	(3. .)
Takahashi:	**A, Sumisu-san.**
Sumisu:	(5. .)
Takahashi:	**Iie, dō itashimashite. Watashitachi mo tanoshikatta desu. Dōzo mata kite kudasai.**
Sumisu:	(8. .)

TRACK
53

EXERCISE

How about Going to a Concert?

Ms. Chan invites Mr. Suzuki to a concert.

Chan: **Asatte Tokyō Hōru de Konsāto ga arimasu. Issho ni ikimasen ka.**

Suzuki: **Ii desu ne. Ikimashō.**

Chan: **Doko de aimashō ka.**

Suzuki: **Roppongi Eki no kaisatsuguchi de aimasen ka.**

Chan: **Ee, sō shimashō.**

①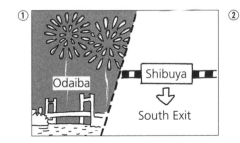

②

TRACK 54 **SHORT DIALOGUE ①**
Won't You Join Us, Ms. Chan?

Ms. Nakamura asks Ms. Chan to join her and Mr. Smith for tennis.

KEY PHRASE   **Chan-san mo issho ni shimasen ka.**

Nakamura: **Raishū Sumisu-san to tenisu o shimasu.**
           (**.)**
Chan: **Arigatō gozaimasu. Zehi.**

SHORT DIALOGUE ⑪
Won't You Come Over?

Mr. Takahashi invites Mr. Smith to his house for a party.

KEY PHRASE **Kimasen ka.**

Takahashi: **Sumisu-san, konshū no nichi-yōbi ni uchi de pātī o shimasu.**
(.)
Sumisu: **Arigatō gozaimasu. Zehi.**

TARGET DIALOGUE

Won't You Go With Me?

Mr. Kato invites Mr. Smith to a festival in Asakusa.

Katō:	Sumisu-san, konshū no do-yōbi ni Asakusa de o-matsuri ga arimasu. Issho ni ikimasen ka.	
Sumisu:	(2.	.)
	(3.	.)
Katō:	Chikatetsu de ikimasen ka.	
Sumisu:	(5.	.)
	(6.	.)
Katō:	Asakusa Eki no kaisatsuguchi de aimasen ka.	
Sumisu:	(8.	.)
	(9.	.)
Katō:	10-ji wa dō desu ka.	
Sumisu:	(11.	.)
	(12.	.)

EXERCISE ①

I'm Sorry, I Have a Meeting Tonight . . .

Mr. Smith invites Ms. Nakamura to a movie.

Sumisu: Eiga no kippu ga 2-mai arimasu. Nakamura-san, komban issho ni ikimasen ka.

Nakamura: Sumimasen, komban <u>kaigi ga arimasu.</u>

Sumisu: Sō desu ka. Ja, mata kondo.

①

②

no time

EXERCISE ⓵

Shall I Lend You My Racket?

Ms. Nakamura invites Ms. Chan to play tennis with her.

ex.

1. next week ?

2.

3. Nakamura

lend ?

4.

Nakamura: Chan-san, raishū issho ni <u>tenisu</u> o shimasen ka.

Chan: Demo, <u>raketto</u> ga arimasen.

Nakamura: Watashi no o kashimashō ka.

Chan: Arigatō gozaimasu. Onegaishimasu.

①

②

SHORT DIALOGUE ①
Are You Okay?

At a festival, Mr. Smith accidentally steps on someone's foot.

KEY PHRASE   Daijōbu desu ka.

onna no hito: **A, itai.**
Sumisu: **A, sumimasen. (.)**
onna no hito: **Ee, daijōbu desu.**
Sumisu: **Dōmo sumimasendeshita.**

SHORT DIALOGUE ⑪
I'm Feeling a Bit Out of Sorts

Mr. Kato calls out to Mr. Smith, who appears to be ill.

KEY PHRASE   **Chotto kibun ga warui n desu.**

Katō: **Daijōbu desu ka.**

Sumisu: **(**   **.)**

Katō: **Asoko ni benchi ga arimasu kara, chotto yasumimashō.**

Sumisu: **Hai.**

TARGET DIALOGUE
Shall I Lend You Mine?

Mr. Smith meets Mr. Suzuki, who is wearing a *happi* coat, and calls out to him.

Katō:	A, Sumisu-san, asoko ni Suzuki-san ga imasu yo.
Sumisu:	(2. .)
	(3. .)
Suzuki:	A, Sumisu-san. Sumisu-san mo issho ni o-mikoshi o katsugimasen ka.
Sumisu:	(6. .)
Suzuki:	Watashi no o kashimashō ka.
Sumisu:	(8. .)
Suzuki:	Ee, watashi wa 2-mai arimasu kara.
Sumisu:	(10. .)

REVIEW 3

Mr. Smith visits Mr. Takahashi's home.

TRACK 62 **EXERCISE**

I'll Go to Kyoto and See a Festival

Mr. Kato asks Mr. Smith what he plans to do after a scheduled meeting.

Katō:	Sumisu-san, kaigi no ato de doko ni ikimasu ka.
Sumisu:	<u>Kyōto</u> ni itte, <u>o-matsuri o mimasu.</u>
Katō:	Sō desu ka.

①

②

SHORT DIALOGUE ①
I'm Getting Some Friends Together for a Party

Mrs. Green is planning a party. She calls up Mrs. Matsui to invite her.

 KEY PHRASE   **Nichi-yōbi ni tomodachi o yonde, pātī o shimasu.**

Gurin: **Nihon-jin no tomodachi ni Kyōto no yūmeina o-sake o moraimashita.**
         (.)
         Matsui-san mo kimasen ka.
Matsui: **Arigatō gozaimasu. Zehi.**

SHORT DIALOGUE ⑪
Why (Not)?

Ms. Nakamura asks Ms. Chan if she plans to attend Mrs. Green's party.

KEY PHRASE Dōshite desu ka.

Nakamura:	Ashita no pātī ni ikimasu ka.
Chan:	Iie, ikimasen.
Nakamura:	(.)
Chan:	Honkon kara haha ga kimasu kara.

TARGET DIALOGUE
I'm Going to the Sapporo Branch Office

Ms. Chan is talking with Ms. Sasaki about her sudden business trip.

Chan: (1.   .)
Sasaki: **Hai.**
Chan: (3.   .)
Sasaki: **Kaigi wa nan-ji kara desu ka.**
Chan: (5.   .)
          (6.   .)
          (7.   .)
Sasaki: **Wakarimashita. Dewa, ki o tsukete.**

EXERCISE ①
Please Deliver This Table to My House

Ms. Chan has purchased an item at a store and asks for it to be delivered to her house.

Chan: Sumimasen. Uchi ni kono <u>tēburu</u> o todokete kudasai.
mise no hito: Hai.
Chan: <u>Do-yōbi ni</u> todokete kudasai.
mise no hito: Hai, wakarimashita. Dewa, o-namae to go-jūsho o onegaishimasu.

① the day after tomorrow P.M.

② by 11:00 Sun.

EXERCISE ⑪
Turn Left at the Next Set of Lights, Please

Mr. Smith is in a taxi. He wants to get within the vicinity of a certain place and must give the driver specific instructions.

Sumisu:	**Shinjuku Eki no chikaku made onegaishimasu.**
untenshu:	**Hai.**
Sumisu:	(*after a while*) **Tsugi no shingō o hidari ni magatte kudasai.**
untenshu:	**Hai.**
Sumisu:	**Ano manshon no mae de tomete kudasai.**
untenshu:	**Hai, wakarimashita.**
untenshu:	(*after a while*) **4,000-en desu.**
Sumisu:	**Hai.**
untenshu:	**Arigatō gozaimashita.**
Sumisu:	**Dōmo.**

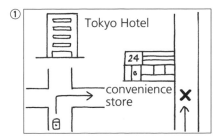

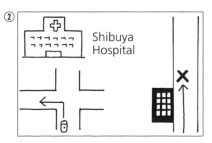

TRACK 68 **SHORT DIALOGUE ①**
Please Bring Me a Blanket

Ms. Chan phones room service because her room is cold.

KEY PHRASE   **Mōfu o mottekite kudasai.**

hoteru no hito: Hai, rūmu-sābisu desu.
Chan: Sumimasen, 201 no Chan desu ga, (.)
hoteru no hito: Hai, wakarimashita.

TRACK 69

SHORT DIALOGUE ⑪
Please Watch Over This Suitcase till Five

Ms. Chan is checking out of the hotel

KEY PHRASE **Kono nimotsu o 5-ji made azukatte kudasai.**

Chan:	Sumimasen.
furonto no hito:	Hai, nan deshō ka.
Chan:	( )
furonto no hito:	Hai, wakarimashita.

TARGET DIALOGUE

Please Send Me the Catalog Right Away

Ms. Chan is in Sapporo attending a sales conference.

Chan:	(1.	.)
Suzuki:	**A, Chan-san, ohayō gozaimasu. Suzuki desu.**	
Chan:	(4.	.)
	(5.	.)
	(6.	.)
Suzuki:	**Hai, wakarimashita.**	
Chan:	(8.	.)
Suzuki:	**Hai, sugu okurimasu.**	
Chan:	(10.	.)

EXERCISE ①
How Long Will You Be in Kyoto?

Ms. Chan asks Mr. Suzuki about his summer vacation plans.

Chan: **Natsu-yasumi ni doko ni ikimasu ka.**
Suzuki: **Kyōto ni itte o-tera o mimasu.**
Chan: **Sō desu ka. Donogurai Kyōto ni imasu ka.**
Suzuki: **itsukakan imasu.**
Chan: **Ii desu ne.**

①

②

EXERCISE ⑪
We'll Leave at Half Past Ten

Ms. Sasaki invites Mr. Smith to a candy expo.

Sasaki: Ashita 11-ji kara <u>Yokohama</u> de o-kashi no fea ga arimasu. Sumisu-san mo issho ni ikimasen ka.

Sumisu: Hai. Nan-ji ni kaisha o demasu ka.

Sasaki: <u>Yokohama</u> made <u>1-jikan han</u> gurai kakarimasu kara, <u>9-ji han</u> ni demasu.

Sumisu: Wakarimashita.

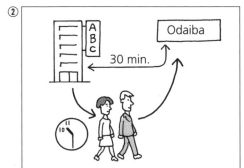

TRACK 73

SHORT DIALOGUE
Yoko—— . . . What Is That?

Mr. Green wants to go to Kamakura.

KEY PHRASE   Yoko—— . . . nan desu ka.

Gurin: Sumimasen, kono densha wa Kamakura ni ikimasu ka.
ekiin: Iie, ikimasen. Yokosuka-sen ni notte kudasai.
Gurin: (.)
ekiin: Yokosuka-sen desu. Chika 1-kai no 1-bansen desu yo.
Gurin: Arigatō gozaimasu.

TRACK 74

TARGET DIALOGUE

What Time Should We Leave the Office?

Ms. Nakamura recently heard that the Sakura Art Museum is open till 8:00 P.M. on Fridays.

Nakamura: Chan-san, ashita shigoto no ato de Sakura Bijutsukan ni ikimasen ka.
Chan: (2.   )
Nakamura: Nan-ji ni kaisha o demashō ka.
Chan: (4.   )
Nakamura: 40-pun gurai kakarimasu.
Chan: (6.   )
Nakamura: Ee. Ja, ashita 6-ji ni.

EXERCISE
May I Have This Pamphlet?

Ms. Chan wants information.

Chan:	Sumimasen, kono <u>ryokan</u> no <u>panfuretto</u> ga arimasu ka.
mise no hito:	Hai, kore desu.
Chan:	Moratte mo ii desu ka.
mise no hito:	Hai, dōzo.

①

restaurant card

②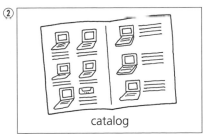

catalog

SHORT DIALOGUE ①
Is It Okay to Write in Romaji?

Mr. Green has gone to the hospital to visit a sick friend. He first goes to the reception desk in the visiting area.

KEY PHRASE **Rōmaji de kaite mo ii desu ka.**

uketsuke: **Go-jūsho to o-namae o kaite kudasai.**

Gurin: **(** **.)**

uketsuke: **Hai.**

SHORT DIALOGUE ⑪
May I Use Your Bathroom?

Mr. Green is visiting a friend.

KEY PHRASE   O-tearai o tsukatte mo ii desu ka.

Gurīn:	**Koko ni nimotsu o oite mo ii desu ka.**
tomodachi:	**Hai, dōzo.**
Gurīn:	*(after chatting for a while)* **Sumimasen. (** .**)**
tomodachi:	**Hai, dōzo.**

TRACK
78

TARGET DIALOGUE
Is It Okay to Take a Picture of the Ukiyoe?

Ms. Chan and Ms. Nakamura are looking at woodblock prints at the Sakura Art Museum. The two of them ask a museum employee some questions.

Nakamura:	Kireina ukiyoe desu ne.	
Chan:	(2.	.)
Nakamura:	Sumimasen. Ukiyoe no shashin o totte mo ii desu ka.	
bijutsukan no hito:	Hai.	
Nakamura:	A, koko ni Eigo no panfuretto ga arimasu yo.	
Chan:	(6.	.)
	(7.	.)
bijutsukan no hito:	Hai, dōzo.	

EXERCISE ①

This Is a Nonsmoking Restaurant . . .

Mr. Smith is at a nonsmoking restaurant when a man sitting close to him lights up a cigarette.

Sumisu: Sumimasen, <u>kono resutoran wa kin'en desu</u> kara, tabako o suwanaide kudasai.

otoko no hito: Hai, wakarimashita. Sumimasen.

EXERCISE ⑪
Don't Put Any Sugar in It

Mr. Smith is ordering at a restaurant.

Sumisu:	Sumimasen, <u>aisu-kōhī</u> o onegaishimasu.
mise no hito:	Hai.
Sumisu:	Sumimasen ga, <u>satō</u> o irenaide kudasai.
mise no hito:	Hai, wakarimashita.

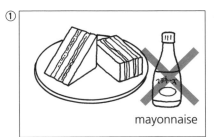

① mayonnaise

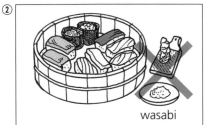

② wasabi

TRACK 81

SHORT DIALOGUE ①

Please Don't Worry about It

Mr. Smith got drunk at the Sasakis' house and spilled red wine on their clean carpet. The next day, he apologizes at the office.

KEY PHRASE Iie, dōzo ki ni shinaide kudasai.

Sumisu: Sasaki-san, kinō wa sumimasendeshita.

Sasaki: (.)

SHORT DIALOGUE ⑪
Okay, I Understand

Mr. Smith goes to a clinic because he has a stomachache.

1. today

2. OK.

KEY PHRASE   Hai, wakarimashita.

isha: Kyō wa o-sake o nomanaide kudasai.

Sumisu: (.)

TARGET DIALOGUE
Please Don't Use a Flash Here

Ms. Chan and Ms. Nakamura are looking at a picture of Mt. Fuji in an art museum.

Chan:	(1. .)
Nakamura:	**Sō desu ne.**
Chan:	(3. .)
Nakamura:	**Hai, wakarimashita. Torimasu yo.** (*takes a flash picture*)
bijutsukan no hito:	**Sumimasen, koko de furasshu o tsukawanaide kudasai.**
Nakamura:	**Sumimasen, wakarimashita.**

Mr. Kato invites Ms. Chan to a party at his home.

NEW WORDS

Hiroo	Hiroo (district in Tokyo)
Hibiya-sen	Hibiya Line (subway line in Tokyo)

Nakameguro	Nakameguro (district in Tokyo)
Tōyoko-sen	Toyoko Line (train line in Tokyo)

NEW WORDS

Tanoshimi ni shite imasu   I'm looking forward to . . .

EXERCISE
I'm Talking to a Client at the Moment

Ms. Chan gets a call on her cell phone from Ms. Matsui. Since she is busy at the moment of the call, she answers quietly.

ex.

1. Ms. Chan?
2. Yes.
3. Matsui
4. Excuse me, but
5. again later
6. Please do.

Matsui:	Moshimoshi, Chan-san desu ka.
Chan:	Hai.
Matsui:	Matsui desu.
Chan:	Matsui-san, sumimasen ga, ima <u>o-kyaku-san to hanashi o shite imasu</u>.
Matsui:	Ja, mata ato de denwa o shimasu.
Chan:	Onegaishimasu.

① Japanese school

おはよう

② meeting

TRACK
85

SHORT DIALOGUE ①
Sorry, Not Yet

Ms. Sasaki is waiting for Ms. Chan's report on her business trip to Hokkaido.

1. already
   report
   ?

2. Sorry, not yet.

3. Please wait a bit more.

KEY PHRASE   **Sumimasen, mada desu.**

Sasaki: **Chan-san, repōto wa mō kakimashita ka.**

Chan: **(.) Mō sukoshi matte kudasai.**

SHORT DIALOGUE ⓫
Since No One Is Using It Now, Go Ahead

Mr. Suzuki is looking for an empty conference room.

 KEY PHRASE   **Ima dare mo tsukatte imasen kara, dōzo.**

Suzuki: Sumimasen. 3-gai no kaigishitsu o tsukatte mo ii desu ka.
Nakamura: Ee. (.)

TRACK
87

TARGET DIALOGUE
Right Now She's Explaining the New Products

Mr. Smith is looking for Ms. Chan. He enters the sales department office and asks Mr. Suzuki where she is.

Sumisu: (1.   .)

Suzuki: Iie. Ima 3-gai no kaigishitsu ni imasu.

Sumisu: (3.   .)

Suzuki: Ima, Nozomi Depāto no Takahashi-san ni atarashii shōhin no setsumei o shite imasu.

Sumisu: (5.   .)

EXERCISE ①
Do You Know Where They Sell . . .?

Mr. Smith is looking to buy certain items.

Sumisu: <u>JBP no atarashii denshi-jisho</u> o shitte imasu ka.

Suzuki: Ee, shitte imasu.

Sumisu: Doko de utte imasu ka.

Suzuki: <u>Shinjuku no denki-ya</u> de utte imasu.

① famous Chinese sweets

Depāto

department store in Yokohama

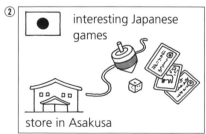

② interesting Japanese games

store in Asakusa

EXERCISE ⅠⅠ
Do You Know Mr. Ando's Phone Number?

Ms. Chan wants to know a certain person's contact details.

Chan: JBP Japan no <u>Andō-san</u> o shitte imasu ka.
Suzuki: Hai, shitte imasu.
Chan: Ja, <u>Andō-san no denwa-bangō</u> o shitte imasu ka.
Suzuki: Iie, shirimasen.

① Mr. Yamashita
JBP Japan
×××–××××–××××

② e-mail
×××@××××.ne.jp
Ms. Kojima
JBP Japan

SHORT DIALOGUE
I'm Not Sure . . .

Mr. Smith wants to make a reservation at the sushi restaurant Sushimasa, but he doesn't know the phone number.

KEY PHRASE   **Sā, wakarimasen.**

Sumisu: **Sumimasen. Sushimasa no denwa-bangō o shitte imasu ka.**

Nakamura: **(.) Suzuki-san ni kiite kudasai.**

TARGET DIALOGUE
I Live in Nagoya

A customer from Nagoya has phoned to inquire about ABC Foods' new products.

Chan: (1.   .)

kyaku: **Sumimasen, ABC Fūzu no atarashii chokorēto wa doko de utte imasu ka.**

Chan: (3.   .)

kyaku: **Ee, sō desu.**

Chan: (5.   .)

kyaku: **Watashi wa Nagoya ni sunde imasu. Nagoya de mo utte imasu ka.**

Chan: (8.   .)

kyaku: **Sō desu ka. Wakarimashita.**

Chan: (10.   .)

EXERCISE ①
Do You Like Italian Food?

Mr. Smith is talking with Ms. Nakamura about his plans.

Sumisu:	Do-yōbi ni <u>Ginza</u> ni itte <u>Itaria ryōri</u> o tabemasu.
Nakamura:	Ii desu ne. Sumisu-san wa <u>Itaria ryōri</u> ga suki desu ka.
Sumisu:	Ee, suki desu. Nakamura-san wa?
Nakamura:	Watashi mo suki desu.
Sumisu:	Ja, kondo issho ni ikimasen ka.
Nakamura:	Arigatō gozaimasu. Zehi.

① Hakone

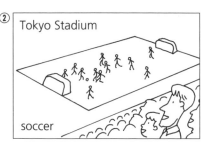

② Tokyo Stadium

soccer

EXERCISE ⑪
Ms. Kojima Speaks Very Good Korean

Ms. Chan is interested in knowing more about a certain person.

Chan: **Katō-san, achira wa donata desu ka.**

Katō: **JBP Japan no Kojima-san desu. Kojima-san wa Kankoku ni sunde imashita kara, Kankoku-go ga totemo jōzu desu.**

Chan: **Sō desu ka. Watashi wa raishū kara Kankoku-go o naraimasu.**

Katō: **Ja, shōkaishimashō ka.**

Chan: **Ee, onegaishimasu.**

①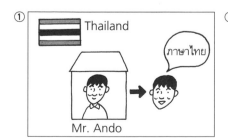

②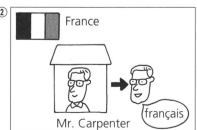

SHORT DIALOGUE
Shall I Introduce You?

Ms. Nakamura is interested in Mr. Ogawa.

1.

2. Mr. Ogawa sometimes

3.

4. ?

5. Yes, please.

 KEY PHRASE   Shōkaishimashō ka.

Nakamura: Gurīn-san, achira wa donata desu ka.

Gurīn: A, Ogawa-san desu. Tokidoki issho ni kendō no renshū o shimasu.

Nakamura: Sō desu ka. Sutekina hito desu ne.

Gurīn: (.)

Nakamura: Ee, onegaishimasu.

TARGET DIALOGUE
Mr. Smith is Very Good at Tennis

The Greens are having a formal party at their house. During the party, Mr. Green introduces Mr. Smith to his friend Mr. Ogawa.

Gurin: (1.   .)

Ogawa: Hajimemashite, Ogawa desu. Yoroshiku onegaishimasu.

Sumisu: ABC Fūzu no Sumisu desu. Yoroshiku onegaishimasu.

Gurin: (7.   .)

       (8.   .)

Ogawa: Sō desu ka. Watashi mo tenisu ga suki desu.

Sumisu: Ja, konshū no do-yōbi ni Ogawa-san mo issho ni tenisu o shimasen ka.

Ogawa: Arigatō gozaimasu. Zehi.

TRACK
96

EXERCISE ①
I, Too, Would Like to Play Golf

Ms. Sasaki tells Mr. Smith what she did over the weekend.

Sasaki: Nichi-yōbi ni <u>gorufu</u> o shimashita.
Sumisu: Ii desu ne. Watashi mo <u>shitai</u> desu.
Sasaki: Ii <u>gorufu-kōsu</u> o oshiemashō ka.
Sumisu: Ee, onegaishimasu.

① Japanese old furniture ... shop

② hot spring

NEW WORDS

gorufu-kōsu   golf course

EXERCISE ⑪
I Didn't Go Because I Had a Fever

Mr. Suzuki asks Ms. Chan whether she went to Mr. White's farewell party.

Suzuki: **Kinō Howaito-san no sōbetsukai ni ikimashita ka.**

Chan: **Iie, ikitakatta desu ga, <u>netsu ga arimashita</u> kara, ikimasendeshita.**

Suzuki: **Sō desu ka. Zannen deshita ne.**

①    ②

SHORT DIALOGUE
Mr. Smith, How about Going Home with Us?

Mr. Green's party has come to an end.

KEY
PHRASE   **Sumisu-san mo issho ni ikaga desu ka.**

Ogawa: **Nakamura-san, kuruma de kimashita ka.**

Nakamura: **Iie, densha de kimashita.**

Ogawa: **Osoi desu kara, watashi no kuruma de kaerimasen ka.**

Nakamura: **Arigatō gozaimasu.**

Ogawa: **(.)**

Sumisu: **Arigatō gozaimasu. Onegaishimasu.**

TARGET DIALOGUE
I, Too, Would Like to Learn Japanese Cooking

Mrs. Green is serving food to Mr. Smith and Mr. Ogawa. Mr. Smith and Mr. Ogawa are eating Japanese food that Mrs. Green made.

Sumisu: (1. .)

Ogawa: Hontō ni oishii desu ne. Gurīn-san wa ryōri ga jōzu desu ne.

Gurīn: Arigatō gozaimasu. Maishū sui-yōbi ni Ginza no kukkingu-sukūru de Nihon-ryōri o naratte imasu.

Sumisu: (6. .)

(7. .)

Gurīn: Nozomi Depāto no tonari ni arimasu.

REVIEW 5

Mr. Kato tells Mr. Smith about his recent visit to Kyoto.

COMPREHENSIVE REVIEW

Imagine that you are visiting the house of a Japanese friend. (Make one up if you don't have one in real life.)

1. Greet the family and introduce yourself.

2. Give the family a gift. Be sure to use appropriate gift-giving expressions.

3. Tell the family about your job—what you do, where you work, etc.—and where you live.

4. Tell the family about your daily routine and what your interests are.

5. Ask the family what their interests are and what they typically do on weekends.

6. At the dinner table, praise the food you have been served.

7. Having been asked what your favorite foods are, explain.

8. Talk about the products or places that your hometown is famous for.

9. Talk about your family—how many members are in it, who they are and where they live or are employed, etc.

10. Tell the family that it is time for you to get going, and thank them for their hospitality.

ANSWERS

Lesson 1

Exercise I
① Katō-san / Katō ② Nakamura-san / Nakamura ③ Suzuki-san / Suzuki ④ Chan-san / Chan

Exercise II
① Gibuson-san / Ōsutoraria Taishikan no Gibuson ② Paku-san / Kankoku Bōeki no Paku ③ Howaito-san / Kanada Shōken no Howaito ④ Ferunandesu-san / Supein Hoken no Ferunandesu

Target Dialogue
3. Hajimemashite. 4. Sumisu desu. 5. Yoroshiku onegaishimasu.

Lesson 2

Exercise
① hon / hon ② kagi / kagi

Target Dialogue
2. Dōmo arigatō gozaimasu. 3. Kore wa Takahashi-san no namae desu ka. 5. Kore wa?

Lesson 3

Exercise
① pūru / gozen 10-ji ② jimu / gozen 8-ji

Target Dialogue
1. Sumimasen, ima nan-ji desu ka. 3. Depāto wa nan-ji kara desu ka. 5. Nan-ji made desu ka. 7. Arigatō gozaimasu.

Lesson 4

Exercise
① bideo kamera / dejikame / bideo kamera / 50,000-en ② terebi /pasokon /terebi / 230,000-en

Target Dialogue
2. Sore o misete kudasai. 4. Arigatō. Kore wa ikura desu ka. 6. Sore wa ikura desu ka. 8. Ja, sore o kudasai.

Lesson 5

Exercise
① wain / wain / Amerika / 3-bon ② kōhī-kappu / kōhī-kappu / Igirisu / yottsu

Target Dialogue
1. Sumimasen. Ano T-shatsu wa ikura desu ka. 3. Ano aoi T-shatsu desu. 5. Sono akai T-shatsu wa ikura desu ka. 7. Ja, sore o 2-mai kudasai.

Review 1-1

1. Takahashi-san,
2. Kochira wa Rondon Ginkō no Buraun-san desu.
3. Hajimemashite.

4. Buraun desu.
5. Yoroshiku onegaishimasu.
6. Hajimemashite.
7. Takahashi desu.
8. Yoroshiku onegaishimasu.
9. Watashi no meishi desu. Dōzo.
10. Dōmo arigatō gozaimasu.
11. Kore wa Takahashi-san no namae desu ka.
12. Ee, sō desu. Takahashi Shingo desu.

Review 1-2

1. Sumimasen. Ano dejikame o misete kudasai
2. Dore desu ka.
3. Ano akai dejikame desu.
4. Hai, dōzo.
5. Arigatō.
6. Kore wa ikura desu ka.
7. 24,800-en desu.
8. Sō desu ka.
9. Sono kuroi dejikame wa ikura desu ka.
10. 19,800-en desu.
11. Ja, sore o kudasai.

Lesson 6

Exercise
① raishū / Chan-san ② asatte / Katō-san

Target Dialogue
1. Moshimoshi, ABC no Sumisu desu. 3. Ashita sochira ni ikimasu. Kaigi wa 3-ji kara desu ne. 6. Iie, kaisha no hito to ikimasu. 8. Shitsureishimasu.

Lesson 7

Exercise
① 10-ji / hikōki ② 8-ji / Shinkansen

Target Dialogue
2. Shitsureishimasu. 5. Arigatō gozaimasu. 7. Iie, chikatetsu de kimashita.

Lesson 8

Exercise
① Odaiba / Odaiba / hoteru ya onsen ② Hakone / Hakone / mizuumi ya onsen

Target Dialogue
2. Sō desu ka. Nikkō ni nani ga arimasu ka. 5. Onsen tte nan desu ka. 8. Ii desu ne.

Lesson 9

Exercise
① chikatetsu no iriguchi / chikatetsu no iriguchi / depāto no naka ② basutei / basutei / ginkō no mae

Target Dialogue
1. Sumimasen. Kono chikaku ni chūshajō ga arimasu ka. 3. Doko desu ka. 6. Dōmo arigatō.

Lesson 10

Exercise
① tomodachi / kaimono / Shibuya   ② Sumisu-san / tenisu / Hakone

Target Dialogue
1. Shūmatsu ni nani o shimasu ka.   3. Sō desu ka.   5. Nichi-yōbi ni Ginza de Suzuki-san to tempura o tabemasu.

Lesson 11

Exercise
① Ginza no depāto / Ginza no depāto / wain   ② Tōkyō Toshokan / Tōkyō Toshokan / eigo no bideo

Target Dialogue
4. Ii mise desu ne.   5. Suzuki-san wa yoku kono mise ni kimasu ka.   8. Suzuki-san, kono sakana wa nan desu ka.   10. Oishii desu ne.

Review 2

1. Sumisu-san wa ABC Fūzu no bengoshi desu.
2. Sumisu-san wa kotoshi no 6-gatsu ni Nihon ni kimashita.
3. Sumisu-san no kaisha wa Tōkyō Eki no chikaku ni arimasu.
4. Shigoto wa getsu-yōbi kara kin-yōbi made desu.
5. Chikatetsu de kaisha ni ikimasu.
6. Kaisha wa mainichi 9-ji kara 6-ji made desu.
7. Hiru-yasumi wa 12-ji han kara 1-ji han made desu.
8. Kaisha no chikaku no resutoran de hiru-gohan o tabemasu.
9. Uchi ni 7-ji goro kaerimasu.

Lesson 12

Exercise I
① atsui / atsui   ② ii tenki / ii tenki   ③ atatakai / atatakai   ④ suzushii / suzushii

Exercise II
① kōban   ② toshokan

Target Dialogue
2. Arigatō gozaimasu.   4. Hai, itadakimasu.   5. Kireina o-kashi desu ne.   6. Nihon no o-kashi desu ka.   8. Totemo oishii desu.   10. Iie, mō kekkō desu.

Lesson 13

Exercise
① Ii tokei / tanjōbi   ② Kireina iyaringu / Kurisumasu

Target Dialogue
1. Kireina kabin desu ne.   3. Ii iro desu ne.

Lesson 14

Exercise I
① Nikkō / Nikkō / Nikkō / kirei deshita   ② Sapporo / Sapporo / Sapporo / samukatta desu

Exercise II
① Katō-san / go-shujin   ② Nakamura-san / Mayumi-san

Target Dialogue

1. Moshimoshi, Takahashi-san no o-taku desu ka.   3. Sumisu desu.   5. Kinō wa dōmo arigatō gozaimashita. Totemo tanoshikatta desu.   8. Dōmo arigatō gozaimasu.

Lesson 15

Exercise

① Odaiba / hanabi-taikai / Shibuya Eki no minamiguchi   ② taishikan / pātī / Tōkyō Eki no nishiguchi

Target Dialogue

2. Ii desu ne. Ikimashō.   3. Nan de ikimashō ka.   5. Sō shimashō.   6. Doko de aimashō ka.   8. Hai.
9. Nan-ji ni aimashō ka.   11. 10-ji desu ne.   12. Ja, do-yōbi ni.

Lesson 16

Exercise I

① eigo no jugyō ga arimasu   ② jikan ga arimasen

Exercise II

① gorufu / kurabu   ② sukī / dōgu

Target Dialogue

2. Hontō desu ne.   3. Suzuki-san.   6. Demo, happi ga arimasen.   8. Ii n desu ka.   10. Arigatō gozaimasu. Ja, onegaishimasu.

Review 3

1. Konnichiwa.
2. Yoku irasshaimashita.
3. Dōzo ohairikudasai.
4. Ojamashimasu.
5. O-cha o dōzo.
6. Arigatō gozaimasu.
7. O-kashi wa ikaga desu ka.
8. Hai, itadakimasu.
9. Kore wa Okinawa no o-kashi desu.
10. Kinō tonari no hito ni moraimashita.
11. Totemo oishii desu.
12. Raishū no do-yōbi wa hima desu ka.
13. Ee.
14. Asakusa de o-matsuri ga arimasu.
15. Issho ni ikimasen ka.
16. Ii desu ne. Zehi.
17. Ja, doko de aimashō ka.
18. Sō desu ne . . .
19. Asakusa Eki no kaisatsuguchi de aimasen ka.
20. Hai.
21. Nan-ji ni aimashō ka.
22. 1-ji wa dō desu ka.
23. Ee. Sō shimashō.
24. Ja, sorosoro shitsurei shimasu.
25. Sō desu ka.
26. A, ame desu ne.
27. Kasa o kashimashō ka. Takusan arimasu kara.
28. Arigatō gozaimasu. Ja, onegaishimasu.
29. Kyō wa dōmo arigatō gozaimashita.
30. Dō itashimashite. Mata kite kudasai.

Lesson 17

Exercise
① Kōbe / sutēki o tabemasu ② Depāto / Ōsaka no o-miyage o kaimasu

Target Dialogue
1. Sasaki-san, chotto yoroshii desu ka. 3. Ashita Hokkaidō de hambai-kaigi ga arimasu kara, Sapporo ni ikimasu. 5. Gozen 10-ji kara gogo 3-ji made desu. 6. Kaigi no ato de Sapporo-shisha ni itte, Satō-san ni aimasu. 7. Asatte Hakodate no chokorēto-kōjō o mite, 1-ji no hikōki de Tōkyō ni kaerimasu.

Lesson 18

Exercise I
① terebi / asatte no gogo ② pasokon / Nichi-yōbi no 11-ji made ni

Exercise II
① Tōkyō Hoteru / migi / kombini no temae ② Shibuya Byōin / hidari / kuroi biru no saki

Target Dialogue
1. Moshimoshi, Chan desu ga, ohayō gozaimasu. 4. Ima Sapporo ni imasu. 5. Sumimasen ga, mēru de atarashii shōhin no katarogu o sugu okutte kudasai. 6. Kaigi de tsukaimasu kara. 8. Sorekara, sampuru no shashin mo okutte kudasai. 10. Ja, onegaishimasu.

Lesson 19

Exercise I
① Itaria / bijutsukan / Itaria / isshūkan ② Nyūyōku / myūjikaru / Nyūyōku / tōkakan

Exercise II
① Tōkyō Hoteru / Tōkyō Hoteru / 1-jikan / 10-ji ② Odaiba / Odaiba / 30-pun / 10-ji han

Target Dialogue
2. Ii desu ne. Ikimashō. 4. Koko kara Sakura Bijutsukan made donogurai kakarimasu ka. 6. Ja, 6-ji ni kaisha o demasen ka.

Lesson 20

Exercise
① resutoran / kādo ② pasokon / katarogu

Target Dialogue
2. Hontō ni kirei desu ne. 6. Sō desu ne. 7. Sumimasen. Kono panfuretto o moratte mo ii desu ka.

Lesson 21

Exercise I
① akachan ga imasu ② kono densha wa kin'en desu

Exercise II
① sandoitchi / mayonēzu ② sushi / wasabi

Target Dialogue
1. Kono Fujisan no e wa totemo kirei desu ne. 3. Nakamura-san, kono e no mae de watashi no shashin o totte kudasai.

1. Moshi moshi, Katō desu ga, Chan-san no o-taku desu ka.
2. A, Katō-san, kombanwa.
3. Chan-san, ashita 6-ji kara uchi de pātī o shimasu. Kimasen ka?
4. Arigatō gozaimasu. Zehi.
5. Ashita wa shigoto ga arimasu kara, 7-ji goro itte mo ii desu ka.
6. Ii desu yo.
7. Eki wa doko desu ka.
8. Yokohama desu. Chan-san wa doko kara kimasu ka.
9. Hiroo kara ikimasu. Yokohama made dōyatte ikimasu ka.
10. Hibiya-sen ni notte, Nakameguro Eki de orite kudasai. Sorekara Tōyoko-sen ni notte, Yokohama Eki de orite kudasai.
11. Hiroo Eki kara Yokohama Eki made donogurai kakarimasu ka.
12. 50-pun gurai desu.
13. Yokohama Eki kara o-taku made dōyatte ikimasu ka.
14. Nishiguchi o dete, hidari ni magatte, massugu itte kudasai.
15. Futatsu-me no shingō o migi ni magatte kudasai. Pan-ya ga arimasu.
16. Watashi no uchi wa pan-ya no tonari desu. Shiroi uchi desu kara, sugu wakarimasu yo.
17. Yokohama Eki kara donogurai kakarimasu ka.
18. Aruite 15-fun gurai desu.
19. Wakarimashita.
20. Ashita, tanoshimi ni shite imasu.
21. Watashi mo tanoshimi ni shite imasu.
22. Ja, mata ashita.
23. Dewa, shitsureishimasu.

Lesson 22

Exercise
① Nihon-go no gakkō de benkyō o shiteimasu   ② kaigi o shiteimasu

Target Dialogue
1. Sumimasen. Chan-san wa imasu ka.   3. Sō desu ka.   5. Sō desu ka. Wakarimashita. Dōmo.

Lesson 23

Exercise I
① Yūmeina Chūgoku no o-kashi / Yokohama no depāto   ② Omoshiroi Nihon no gēmu / Asakusa no mise

Exercise II
① Yamashita-san / Yamashita-san no keitai no bangō   ② Kojima-san / Kojima-san no mēru adoresu

Target Dialogue
1. Hai, ABC Fūzu de gozaimasu.   3. "Shokora-shokora" desu ka.   5. Tōkyō no sūpā to kombini de utte imasu.   8. Iie, Nagoya de wa utte imasen. Mōshiwake gozaimasen.   10. Taihen mōshiwake gozaimasen.

Lesson 24

Exercise I
① Hakone / gorufu o shimasu / gorufu   ② Tōkyō sutajiamu / sakkā o mimasu / sakkā

Exercise II
① Andō-san / Andō-san / Tai / Tai-go / Tai-go   ② Kāpentā-san / Kāpentā-san / Furansu / Furansu-go / Furansu-go

Target Dialogue

1. Sumisu-san, kochira wa Ogawa-san desu.   7. Ogawa-san, watashi wa Sumisu-san to maishū do-yōbi ni tenisu o shite imasu.   8. Sumisu-san wa tenisu ga totemo jōzu desu.

Lesson 25

Exercise I

① Nihon no furui kagu o kaimashita / kaitai / mise   ② onsen ni ikimashita / ikitai / onsen

Exercise II

① atama ga itakatta desu   ② ha ga itakatta desu

Target Dialogue

1. Oishii desu ne.   6. Watashi mo Nihon-ryōri o naraitai desu.   7. Sono kukkingu-sukūru wa doko ni arimasu ka.

Review 5

1. Kore wa Kyōto no o-kashi desu.
2. Ikaga desu ka.
3. Hai, itadakimasu.
4. Senshū kazoku to Kyōto ni itte, kaimashita.
5. Oishii desu ne.
6. Kore wa Tōkyō de mo utte imasu ka.
7. Iie, Tōkyō de wa utte imasen.
8. Sō desu ka. Wakarimashita.
9. Kirei desu ne. Kore wa Kyōto desu ka.
10. Hai, sō desu. Gion-matsuri no shashin desu.
11. O-matsuri wa dō deshita ka.
12. Totemo omoshirokatta desu. Nigiyaka deshita yo.
13. Kyōto wa donna tokoro desu ka.
14. Yūmeina jinja ya furui o-tera ga arimasu. Ii tokoro desu yo.
15. Tōkyō kara Kyōto made donogurai kakarimasu ka.
16. Shinkansen de 2-jikan gurai desu.
17. Sō desu ka.
18. Yasumi no hi ni zehi ikitai desu.

Comprehensive Review (sample answer)

1. Konnichiwa. Sumisu desu. Yoroshiku onegaishimasu.
2. Kore o dōzo. Wain/Kēki/Aisukurīmu desu.
3. Watashi wa bengoshi desu. ABC Fūzu ni tsutomete imasu. ABC Fūzu wa Tōkyō Eki no chikaku ni arimasu. Akasaka ni sunde imasu.
4. 9-ji kara 6-ji made kaisha de shigoto o shimasu. Shigoto wa totemo isogashii desu. Tokidoki shigoto no ato de tomodachi to shokuji o shimasu. Shūmatsu ni yoku eiga o mimasu. Watashi wa ryokō ga suki desu. Kyonen wa Kyōto ya Nara ya Kamakura ni ikimashita. Natsu-yasumi ni Hokkaidō ni ikitai desu.
5. Supōtsu/Ongaku ga suki desu ka. Donna supōtsu/ongaku ga suki desu ka. Eiga o yoku mimasu ka. Shūmatsu ni nani o shimasu ka.
6. Totemo oishii desu. Ryōri ga jōzu desu ne.
7. Sushi ya tempura ga suki desu.
8. Watashi wa Amerika no Sanfuranshisuko (San Francisco) kara kimashita. Sanfuranshisuko ni yūmeina Gōruden Gēto Burijji (Golden Gate Bridge) ga arimasu. Fisshāmanzu Wāfu (Fisher-man's Wharf) no shīfūdo (seafood) wa totemo oishii desu yo. Sanfuranshisuko wa totemo ii tokoro desu.
9. Watashi no kazoku wa 4-nin desu. Chichi to haha to ani to watashi desu. Chichi to haha wa Sanfuranshisuko ni sunde imasu. Ani wa Nyūyōku (New York) ni sunde imasu. Ginkō ni tsu-tomete imasu.
10. Ja, sorosoro shitsureishimasu. Kyō wa dōmo arigatō gozaimashita. Totemo tanoshikatta desu.

（改訂第3版）コミュニケーションのための日本語 第1巻 ワークブック
JAPANESE FOR BUSY PEOPLE I: The Workbook for the Revised 3rd Edition

2006 年9月　第 1 刷発行
2008 年1月　第 3 刷発行

著　者　　社団法人 国際日本語普及協会
挿　画　　角 愼作
発行者　　富田 充
発行所　　講談社インターナショナル株式会社
　　　　　〒112-8652 東京都文京区音羽 1-17-14
　　　　　電話　03-3944-6493（編集部）
　　　　　　　　03-3944-6492（営業部・業務部）
　　　　　ホームページ　www.kodansha-intl.com
印刷・製本所　大日本印刷株式会社